MIRACLE MARRIAGE

I forgive you. I trust you. I believe you

Volume 1

JJ AND TRINA HAIRSTON

GODZCHILD PUBLICATIONS

Published by Godzchild Publications
a division of Godzchild, Inc.
22 Halleck St., Newark, NJ 07104
www.godzchildproductions.net

Printed in the United States of America 2019 - 1st Edition

Library of Congress Cataloging-in-Publications Data
Miracle Marriage: I forgive you. I trust you. I believe you/
JJ and Trina Hairston

ISBN-13 978-1-937391-36-2
e-ISBN 978-1-937391-35-5

1. Trina Hairston 2. JJ Hairston

2019

TABLE OF
Contents

Dedication

I'd like to dedicate this book to a wife who is desperate to see change in her marriage.

You might have been advised to leave your marriage. You may have been told that there is no hope. My question is, have you considered what God said? You see, I know when trouble comes into marriages, there is a ton of advice being offered. Sometimes so much advice that it leads you to feel confused and conflicted. That is the time that you have to turn a deaf ear to what everyone is saying and hear God for yourself. Undoubtedly, you have people around you who feel they have your best interest at heart, but truthfully, only God has designed your future. And only he can answer with certainty what is best for you.

Truth be told I was you. I was the (then) girl who sat confused not knowing what do to. I was the one who had people advising me to leave, justifiably so, but when I laid my head down at the end of the night, a still, quiet, but vivacious voice would speak to me. This voice would tell me to hold on.

I now know that this was the Spirit of the Lord. You may hear that voice. You may sense that urge to keep fighting like I did. If so, this book was written just for you! Be encouraged by the words that you read. Be confident that God is no respecter of persons. What it did for me, he will do for you! - *Trina*

I'd like to dedicate this book to husbands who have issues with forgiveness. I pray that, through our testimony, you can be inspired and encouraged to let go of the past, embrace what is, and look forward to what is to come. - *JJ*

INTRODUCTION: THE BEST WINE

Miracles are possible. Miracles are proven. In scripture, Jesus performed over 40 miracles, and in the Old Testament there are over 60 miracles. That tells us that there are over 100 miraculous events in scripture, and if you are in need of a miracle, you can have it! But do you know what is even more amazing to me than that? When I look at the New Testament miracles, I am amazed by the order that they come in. Whatever is done first, is often the thing that takes priority. With that in mind, isn't it interesting that the first miracle was at a wedding? Isn't it interesting that Jesus performed his first miracle at a sacred event where a husband was joining in holy matrimony with his wife?

Most of us know the story of Jesus turning water into wine, but for those who have never read it, here is a brief recap. In John 2, a wedding is happening at Cana. Jesus is there, his disciples are there, and his mother is there. As is the custom during those days, wine was served at this wedding; but when the wine ran out, the people began to panic. Jesus tells the servants to fill the jars with water, and then to draw some water out from the jars they had just filled. At his command, they do what he says, and out from the very jar that just had water in it seconds ago, comes wine. My favorite line in John 2 is this: "what Jesus did here in Cana of Galilee was the first of the signs through which he revealed his glory; and his disciples believed in him" (John 2:11).

When I read this story, I see so much more than water and wine. I see so much more than a party and a prayer. I see how deeply Jesus loved marriage. You see, the shortage of wine, in those days, was humiliating. It was almost like someone coming to your house without you having enough food for them to eat. Or, like going to Dunkin Donuts and they don't have Donuts. The moment people saw you in the street, they would remember that you weren't prepared. They would remember that your wedding was the "ghetto wedding." They would remember that you were too broke to afford this ceremony, and Jesus didn't want the bad press to get in the way of this sacred covenant. He loved that couple so much that he covered them in their shortage. He made up the difference because he knew, that every marriage would come up short somewhere. Jesus didn't want others to look at them disgracefully. So he performed this miracle to protect the image of marriage. I know the world has its own view of marriage, and I know that modern culture has a way of tainting and perverting the images of God-ordained marriages, but let me make sure you are clear about this one true but simple point: *God loves marriage.* God values covenant. Marriage was so important to God that he included it in the first part of creation. He loved marriage so much that the one thing he said was not good, was for man to be alone. So he created help so that we could see, from the beginning, the miracle of marriage. It was never God's intent for marriage to have a bad reputation. Why? Because marriage was designed to represent his undying and unwavering love for us, his church. Marriage was designed to show the world the extent God would go for us, no matter how far away we drifted. When marriages look bad in the world, it misrepresents God's original intent for the church to look like Christ. So, every time God does a miracle in your marriage, trust me, it's about you…but it's about more than you. It's about your children but it's about so much more than your children. It's about your future but it's about more than your future. When God does a miracle in our marriages, it is because he wants to do a miracle in the world. He wants us to look like the masterpiece he created us to be; so that our marriages, like that miracle in John 2, can reveal God's glory in us.

Maybe you are reading this, and your marriage is perfect. You have no issues. Your husband secures you. Your wife honors you. Your children earn straight A's in school, and they are on their way to seminary next year. If that is you, I want to say KUDOS! You are reflecting the image of God in your marriage, and I would still encourage you to keep reading because the longer you live, the quicker you'll realize that seasons change. But if I had to take a wild guess, I would guess that most of us do not have a perfect marriage. Most of us have run out of wine. Most of us are trying to keep it all together, but our weeks are filled with highs and lows—and depending on the day, we just don't know if we can keep doing this, like this.

Trust me, I get it. As you continue to read these books, you will learn that I am a very honest person. And honestly speaking, I remember the days when I couldn't celebrate my marriage. I remember the days when our actions (along with the opinions, speculations, and accusations of others) leaked us dry. We had no joy. We had no peace. We had no wine, and we needed a miracle. Things began to get really bad. Everything wasn't "the devil." Some things were the result of poor planning and bad decisions, but it got

> *Some miracles are not immediate; they are incremental.*

so bad, that I had no one else to turn to but God. I needed God to take what was left and turn it into something valuable. I needed a renovation, a celebration, and reconciliation. I needed the sanctity of my marriage to be observed by the Master and preserved by His sovereignty. I needed healing, relief, and satisfaction. I didn't want to fake the funk. I wanted my smile to be real. And I'm writing this book to tell you without question: God did it. God reconciled us. God reconnected us. God rejuvenated our marriage, and it did not happen immediately, but it did happen eventually. This taught me an important lesson. Some miracles are not immediate; they are incremental. Some miracles are like the 10 lepers who had to leave Jesus' presence and walk toward their healing; and as they went, they were healed. For some of you reading, you may want God to do it quickly—and he is God. He can do anything. But very often, we are asking God to work on our time, not His time. And anything worth saving, takes time. God reconnected us so that we could help others to see that reconciliation is possible. God is no respecter of persons. What God did for us, he

> *As you evaluate where you are in your marriage, answer me this: is Christ in your marriage?*

can do for you. But it begins with you admitting to God, "I'm out of wine." I'm out of options. I'm out of ideas. I'm out of oil. I'm out of it. As you admit where you are, I believe God will take what is left of your marriage and turn it into a celebration worthy of the best wine.

Is Christ In Your Marriage?

As I read this miracle in John 2 over and over again, a few principles jumped out at me that I want to share with you. The first one might be so simple that it can easily be overlooked. Jesus didn't just happen to be in Cana at the time of the wedding. *No, he was invited.* He and his disciples were asked to come to the wedding, and his presence is what made all of the difference.

As you evaluate where you are in your marriage, answer me this: is Christ in your marriage? Has he been invited into the day-to-day affairs of your life? Did you invite him to the wedding, but ignore him during the marriage? Was he present a few years ago, but no longer active now? In order to answer these questions, you're going to have to really be honest with yourself and with your spouse. Because the Bible says "a cord of three strands is not quickly broken" Ecclesiastes 4:12. Is it possible that things are breaking in your marriage because the third strand (God) is missing?

When JJ and I got married, we were very young. Neither of us were capable of handling marriage on our own. In hindsight, I now recognize a lot of things. Firstly, I didn't know who I was. Secondly, I didn't know how to learn and adapt to someone else. Thirdly, we were not adequately prepared for the problems that would soon arise in our marriage. We had three strikes that pointed to imminent divorce, but we decided to invite Jesus into our marriage.

Two people can be saved and sanctified, and still married without Jesus. By that I mean, you can serve the Lord on your own, and you can be a member of a church, singing in the choir and all of that—but if two people are not committed to Christ being over their marriage, then it will be very hard to stay married. Like the wedding in Cana, Christ's presence meant everything. It was not enough for us to hang up scriptures on the walls of our home. We needed those scriptures to live in our hearts. I needed to learn how to be quick to hear and slow to speak. I needed to learn how to love my husband the way he needed to be loved, not necessarily the way I needed him to love me. I needed Jesus to really lead us, and in order to do that, we both had to ask Christ to come in and teach us how to do marriage *His way*.

Miracles require you to be teachable. I've never seen an arrogant person receive a miracle. I've never seen an entitled group receive a miracle. When you realize you can't do this on your own, it is a humbling experience. It will require divine

> *It's one thing to invite Jesus into your marriage, but the hard thing will be to do what he says.*

intervention and your willingness to let Jesus take the wheel. When things got rocky for us at the beginning of our troubled stages, I recall being the only one who wanted the marriage to work. I recall feeling like I was trying and trying, and my husband didn't seem interested the way I was interested. But I had to accept a hard lesson: I didn't have the power to change JJ's mind. The only thing I could do was make the atmosphere conducive for God to work a miracle. Remember this: a miracle isn't needed if man can do it. Miracles are performed when we realize our limitations.

In John 2, Mary knew the feast was going to fail without Jesus' intervention. So, she gathered all of the right players and after asking Jesus for help, she told them, "Do what Jesus said." It's one thing to invite Jesus into your marriage, but the hard thing will be to do what he says. Can you do what Jesus says even

if that means you have to come home earlier
than you used to? Can you do what Jesus says
even if that means you have to check-in during
the middle of your work day? Can you do what
Jesus says when you have to share your expenses
with your spouse? Can you do what Jesus says
when what he says, makes you uncomfortable?
I read a question in a book a few years ago that
messed me up. It said, "What if God designed
marriage not to make us happy, but to make us
holy?" *Ouch.* What if marriage is about more
than sex, smiles, and satisfaction? I don't know
about you, but I would hope that my marriage
included those three areas in abundance, but
my point is: what if God intended marriage
to be about more than those things? What if
marriage was about something greater? What
if it was meant to be a witness to the world that
the same way I love my husband, Christ loves
the church. And the same way my husband loves
me, Christ loves the church. What if marriage
was supposed to be a billboard of God's grace
to a hopeless world?

If you want to see a miracle in your marriage, you must begin to see marriage differently. For starters, I had to see that the outcome of my marriage had a lot to do with my interactions with my spouse. That meant, to the best of my ability, I had to work so that every encounter was as peaceable as possible. Every conversation was as loveable as possible. In order to make sure that happened, I had to prepare myself, my home, and my family for the miracle I was asking God for. I had to put all of the proper elements in place so that God would be welcomed to manifest his presence in my marriage. As you consider your marriage, and where you are right now, I want to encourage you to invite Him in. Once He's in, allow him to take control. When he takes control, let him guide you into what is necessary for your marriage to grow, and most importantly, do what He says.

Who Is on Your Guest List?

As I continued to read the story at the wedding of Cana, it occurred to me that Jesus wasn't the only one invited to the party. The couple had a guest list at this wedding, and usually a guest list is comprised of people who mean something to you. This got me to thinking,

> *Who are you inviting into your marriage? When your marriage is in trouble, who do you call?*

who exactly was on the guest list at this wedding? Were these friends? Were these associates? Did they worship together? Were they close? Then I started asking deeper questions. Out of all of the people invited, why wasn't someone in place to watch the wine? Why didn't they have one person on their list to warn them when things got low? Did their guests drink responsibly, or were they the overindulgent type? Ultimately, it is the responsibility of the bride and groom to appoint someone to manage what is being poured out—I know—but for the purpose of this section, I need to ask you: who are you inviting into your marriage? When your marriage is in trouble, who do you call? Who is looking out for you, checking on you, and praying for you?

Naturally, everyone wants to talk to someone who understands their situation. But if I'm honest, I have had too many conversations with the wrong people in the past. Before I knew any better, I allowed a lot of "guests" to give me unwarranted feedback. They would lead with "if I were you, I would," and that was the problem: they weren't me. But this taught me something important. Every time you engage with someone about your marriage, picture yourself pouring an expensive glass of wine into a glass. The more you talk, the more people can get drunk off of your story. The more you talk, the more they can become intoxicated by the drama and distracted by the story. So, if you decide to talk about your situation, only talk with those who are sober minded. Talk to people who can replenish your marriage. Talk to people who will say the right thing (not the thing you want to hear) and those who will offer the kind of advice that will steer you in the right direction. *The goal is a miracle.* If your guests don't have the same goal, stop inviting them to the wedding. Change the company you keep. Pray for God to send you people in your life who are faith-driven. Ask God to bring people who will hold you accountable

> *If you want a miracle, you have to be willing to do the work.*

to your actions. Every marriage needs mentors who will listen to your heart and direct you back to the arms of Jesus.

A Willingness to Serve

Here is one last nugget from the miracle wedding in John 2.

> *Mary asked Jesus for help.*
> *Jesus asked the servants to pour.*

This is so important. Jesus knew he was responsible for the miracle, but the people were responsible for the work. Jesus never touched the water pots. Instead, the servants filled the pots with water. The servants obeyed Jesus when he spoke, and they didn't object to his command. Here is the point: marriage takes work. If you want a miracle, you have to be willing to do the work. I know what culture says, and most times, people will tell you, "If it's meant to be, it will be." But don't be misled by cute clichés. This saying has made many people lackadaisical in their marriage. This saying has convinced us that we don't have to do the work, because whatever was meant to happen, is going to happen with or without us. But that isn't true for all areas of our lives. We can have all the groceries in the kitchen, but the food won't cook itself. We have to work. We can have a tank full of gas, but the car won't move until we drive. In the same way, our miracle won't happen unless we are willing to do the work. Sure we must depend on God, but that does not mean we do not have a part to play.

Yes, God intended for you to stay together. Yes, God ordained marriage and no marriage is perfect. Yes, God is able to do above what you may ask or think, but God will not fix anything you are not willing to work on. Your effort invites his miracle. Your faith without works is dead. If you want to see God raise your marriage from the dead, you must be willing to do the work.

This is proven throughout scripture, but I want to point to a few quick examples. Consider the woman with the issue of blood. She wanted a miracle of healing. But she couldn't receive that healing inside of her house. So, she fought through the crowd and crawled toward Jesus to touch his hem. Immediately, she was healed. She did her job and Jesus did his. Consider the man who was born blind in John 9. He wanted healing from his blindness. And Jesus could've done all of the work. But instead, he tells the man to go and wash the mud off of his face at a pool called Siloam. When he did the work, he was healed. Consider the man who was an invalid for thirty-eight years. Jesus asked him a question that many of us overlook: *Do you want to be healed?* Because Jesus knew something that most of us ignore: you can give people many things, but you can't give them a *want to*. The invalid gives excuses, at first, but then Jesus tells the man to work: take up your bed and walk. When the man obeys, he is healed. You see: the one commonality in all of these miracles is work. We have to be willing to do the work, and if we do our part, then God will provide the miracle. When we provide the sacrifice, then God will provide the solution. But we must do the work.

So, here are a few questions I'd like you to think about. What work do you need to do in your marriage? What haven't you done that you need to do? Before you look at your spouse's inabilities, what is God asking *you* to do? What have you stopped doing that you need to start doing again? The servants at the wedding obeyed Jesus, and as a result, they witnessed water turn into wine. I wonder what God can transform if you are willing to take on a servant's heart.

As you begin this journey, I pray that God will give you the tools to avoid divorce. I pray that God will give you wisdom and grace to extend forgiveness. I pray that you will experience divine reconciliation. I pray that God will give you and your spouse a "want to." I pray that, together, you will be willing to use these tools appropriately in order to see the change you desire to see for your marriage. Most of all, I pray that God will fill your marriage with **the best wine.**

Introduction: The Best Wine

Marriage, in itself, is a miracle. When you think about two people coming from two families, with two different backgrounds and two different upbringings, and now they are becoming one, that is definitely a miracle. It's a natural miracle and a spiritual one. When God sees married couples, He sees our relationship with him. People see two people who like to take pictures together. People see an image of marriage that may be boring, or less adventurous than the "free life" of singles. But God sees the best kind of love imaginable. God sees how deep he will go to find us, and bring us back to him. No matter how many times we mess up, and no matter how many times we fall short, God is committed to us. He stays connected to us no matter what. This is the ultimate representation of how God loves the church—through the symbol, image, and commitment of a husband and wife. Through marriage, God shows his covenant to the world.

I knew this intellectually, but I started to see it differently when I actually got married. When Trina and I first got married, we didn't understand how important covenant really was. We jumped into marriage for the benefits of covenant: sex. I'm not going to sugarcoat it; I'm going to be honest with you. We wanted to have sex. So, we decided to get married because we wanted to have sex and not be convicted. But I wish I knew before what I know now. I now know that sex is a benefit of the covenant, sex is not the covenant itself. Sex is an expression of love, but it is not the only way to express love. Despite our premature decision and despite our one-sided motivation, God forgave us. God taught us how to honor one another. I admit: we've both done things that were unforgiveable. We've both been told by family members and friends to give up and move on. We've both been encouraged to find happiness somewhere else. But God kept us together after all of these years—and that is simply a miracle.

What's even more amazing is that some of the very people who told us to give up on our marriage, are now coming to us for counseling. They saw our marriage recover. They saw our marriage bounce back. They knew we were contemplating divorce and were living separate lives, but thanks be to God, we are here writing this book, 25 years later and three children later, to tell you—if God did a miracle for us, He can do one for you.

SURVIVING INFIDELITY

If I'm the odd ball out on this debate, I'll settle for being the minority, but as for me and my husband, our marriage is worth fighting for. Granted, we have been married for over 25 years, but in the early part of our marriage, I felt a lot of pressure to get a divorce. People told me I had a right to do so, and even though I didn't necessarily have an unction from God, it was hard to ignore the voices of those we loved and respected. These were rational people (Christian men and women) advising me to let it all go. Many wanted me to leave *my* marriage because (I think) they were projecting onto us something that was going on in *their* marriage. I didn't know it at the time, but some had dealt with infidelity and did not see changes in their marriage

> *At the end of the day, we have the choice to fight or to take flight.*

after fighting, so I think they assumed fighting wasn't going to bring the results I was looking for either. I was young. I was impressionable. But I still didn't subscribe to the idea that "once a cheater, always a cheater." I believed God could heal anyone from anything—and I still do! I believed that God ordained marriage, and the enemy arranged distractions! But at the end of the day, we have the choice to fight or to take flight.

Many days, I found myself sad and nervous. Many days, I wondered if this would actually work out. But deep within my being, I had hope that my marriage was not going to end. What I learned during that time was to magnify the voice of God and minimize the voice of people. The people who were speaking to me, meant well (for

> *When someone's heart is broken, every touch is not consistent with the touch of God. Some bring healing. Some bring more harm.*

the most part), but their advice was not coming from a place of faith. When someone's heart is broken, every touch is not consistent with the touch of God. Some bring healing. Some bring more harm. Now that I am on the other side of the most difficult seasons of my marriage, I can say—without question—staying in your marriage is a decision worth fighting for.

The Outsider

When reading the story of Sarah and Hagar in the Bible, my eyes were opened! Sarah struggled with impatience. She was so anxious about seeing a miracle happen, that she began to arrange things outside of God's instructions. She took it upon herself to orchestrate the "situation" between Abraham, her husband, and Hagar, her servant. One would think Sarah created a monster and had to live with it. But thank God he has mercy on us all! What I love about God is despite our poor decisions, he is faithful to keep His promise.

When we first meet Hagar, we meet a submissive handmaid. She knew that Sarah was in charge, and she respected her authority. When Sarah told her to conceive a child with Abraham, she obeyed. When Sarah told her to clean around the house, she obeyed. But when Hagar became pregnant, she changed. Isn't it funny how people change up on you when they finally get what you've been longing for? Hagar switched from submissive to arrogant. She began to think more highly of herself than she should've—all because she was able to do what Sarah could not.

Look at Hagar now. She's haughty, egotistical, and entitled. Sarah, on the other hand, is furious. In Sarah's mind, Hagar had one job—to serve as a surrogate for Sarah's family. But that arrangement turned into a catastrophe. Sarah was Abraham's wife, and that was never going to change—no matter what Hagar tried to do inside the home.

This should be encouraging to many of us reading today. What Sarah's story teaches me is that an outsider doesn't have the power to change your position as a wife. Even if a mistress has been involved in your marriage, they can never be a wife to *your husband*. They do not have the spiritual, legal or natural authority to take what doesn't belong to them. Hagar might've been pregnant, but her

> *Even if a mistress has been involved in your marriage, they can never be a wife to your husband.*

child did not change her status in God's eyes and in Sarah's house. In their home, she was still a handmaid.

For every wife who has dealt with the threat of a mistress, here is good news for you. Do not let your esteem trick you. Do not allow your feelings to control you. Your calling, as his wife, belongs to one person—**you**. No matter what happened, the infraction does not change your authority in God's eyes. You are who God says you are. When I realized this, it was a game changer for me! I realized that God had given me the authority to reclaim my marriage for His glory, and I was not going to let my husband die "under the influence." I was not going to let an outsider destroy us from the inside. I decided to

BE the wife that God assigned me to be, because I was the only one, by law, who had the covenantal responsibility to cover and protect him.

Wake UP!

When Sarah came to herself, she started laying down the law in a heavy way. I wonder if the mistress will lose her influence once we "come to ourselves"? I wonder if the mistress will lose her power once we start walking in ours? Once Sarah woke up, Hagar walked out. Eventually, she fled the home, and the angel stopped her from walking away. But why? Why did the angel instruct her to go back to the house and submit to Sarah?

Many theologians and preachers have given their opinion about this, and one undeniable reason is because God is a God of order. If Hagar was to receive the blessing promised to her, she would have to complete her assignment and stay connected to Abraham. But there could be another reason why Hagar went back— ☺ You see, when I read the Bible, I use my full imagination. If

Hagar had stormed off and left Abraham's house, imagine the story she would've told her family and friends back home. Remember, she was already a different person. Her arrogance and ego would've painted a picture of God's covenantal family in the wrong light. She would've focused on all the wrong things. In addition to that, imagine the additional scandals that would've hit their home. *Wealthy and successful Abraham and Sarah left poor Hagar to walk, on foot, in a desert.* No food. No home. All left alone. Without a friend. And... get this...she left a wealthy man's house! Boy, the paparazzi would've had a field day!!!! The "scroll news" of that day would have Abraham and Sarah-on-repeat, and the intent of God would've been lost beneath the drama of a good gossip story. People would've asked questions. People would've made assumptions. I believe, God stopped Hagar from leaving for the same reason Jesus stopped the wine from running out

> *God cares about our marriages. He wants the world to see the savior, not the scandal.*

in the wedding at Cana—to protect the image and sanctity of marriage. God cares about our marriages. He wants the world to see the savior, not the scandal. In my opinion, God was sending Hagar back to cover up the hasty decision of Sarah, the poor discernment of Abraham, and the messy business that sometimes happens before the miracle shows up. Why? Because *God is married to the backslider.*

Sin Must Become Subject

This story in Genesis is a perfect demonstration of a larger lesson. Every sin must become subject to the order of God. God is a God of order, and even when we work out of order, God can still turn our mess-ups into a miracle. What I learned, personally, is that I didn't have to leave my marriage because of sin. No, sin had to leave my marriage because of God. Eventually, sin had to obey God's divine order and submit to the Creator of our covenant. Sin won't win when we refuse to give in. In all things God ordained, God's law shall prevail. God has given you the authority to be your husband's wife. God has given you the authority to be your wife's husband. When I coupled this with the discovery of how much God loves

> *When your fight matches God's faith, anything is possible to those who believe.*

marriage, I was empowered to keep fighting. I was recharged. I was given the tools to survive this test. Yes, the odds were against me, but I fought. Yes, the negative words of critics were around me, but I fought. I fought even when JJ couldn't fight. And I have heard many people say that in order for a relationship to survive, both the husband and the wife have to want it. But may I offer you a different perspective? All you truly need is your fight and your faith, and when your fight matches God's faith, anything is possible to those who believe.

Got Faith?

In one season of our lives, my husband no longer wanted to be married. Not only did he tell me he wanted a divorce, but he went as far as picking up divorce papers and filling them out. Back then, this was not a quick process. Divorce papers weren't available online in a downloadable format. No, JJ had to physically travel to the courthouse, obtain the documents, wait in line, drive all the way back home, and initiate the process. He was serious about this thing! Unbeknownst to me, he had filled out the paperwork, and there was nothing I could've done to change his mind.

Many of us try to devise a plan to keep a man. We try to feed him until he is satisfied because we think "a way to a man's heart is through his belly." *Tried it—didn't work.* We even try to put IT on him really good ☺ so that he keeps coming back." *I tried that too, and it somewhat worked.* But truthfully, all of these gimmicks were not long-lasting. They were my attempts to make my marriage work—but none of these things had anything to do with what God said about marriage.

So what was it? What was it that kept JJ from filing those papers? I believe God helped me to change the way I interacted with him. Instead of showing my anger, I prayed for peace to withstand. I stopped complaining

> *An inward change brings outward results.*

and criticizing. I showed him the love of Christ. I accepted him as he was. I didn't force Jesus down his throat—I didn't preach to him—I just *became* love-in-action. I decided to become a witnessing tool for the sake of my marriage. What I learned is this: if you desire it, you can lead your spouse back to the will of God and to the love of Jesus by your actions. An inward change brings outward results. God had to give JJ an inner desire to want this, too. I was his wife, but even greater than that, I was a witness. God used my witness to draw JJ back to himself. And with much prayer and patience, God restored us completely. It took time, but while God was searching his heart, I had to search my own. I took the time to really find Trina. I took the time to ask myself different questions. I took the time to pay attention to things that were not lovely about me. Most importantly, I took the time to make sure I was ready for what I was asking God for.

Was I really ready to forgive?

Was I really ready to let go?

If he confided in me about everything, would I judge him and punish him later?

Was my atmosphere conducive for receiving the miracle I had been praying for?

These are the questions I encourage you to ask yourself. As you pray for the miracle, make sure you are also prepared for the process.

Romans 5:8–But God demonstrates his own love for us in this: while we were still sinners, Christ died for us.

Are you willing to SACRIFICE?

Here are some practical lessons JJ and I learned about infidelity and unconditional love. First, know this: when love is in full demonstration, great sacrifice automatically follows. I have learned in my marriage, that everything may not be my fault, but as a married couple, it is still my responsibility. With that in mind, I know you may have been the faithful partner in your marriage, but my question is: what sacrifices are you willing to make in order to position your marriage

> *The work of reconciliation is a mutual commitment to move forward together, grow together, and heal together.*

toward reconciliation? You may not be the culprit, but surviving infidelity is going to require, both you and your spouse, to do the work. I say that because sometimes we think that the only person who needs to change is the person who committed the act. But the work of reconciliation is a mutual commitment to move forward together, grow together, and heal together.

Don't allow yourself to get too comfortable in a broken place – Some years ago, I thought it was a good idea to wear flip flops for most of the summer months. One day, I developed a shooting pain at the bottom of my foot. I didn't think much of it at first. It was just a temporary inconvenience. I chalked it up to a charlie horse of some kind, and kept it moving. But the pain got worse. Eventually, I had to go to the doctor, and when I was examined, I found out that my arch had collapsed due to wearing shoes for months without arch support. In order to fix that problem, I had to have surgery. During the procedure, the doctor had to take ligaments from other parts of my foot and calf muscles to create a new arch in the place where I had lost strength. I had to wear a cast for several months to ensure that my new ligaments would grow together. Imagine what it must've been like to sit in a cast for six weeks. The surgery was one thing; but the recovery was a different situation altogether. Come to think of it, I was in more pain after the surgery than I was during the surgery! Antibiotics were given to me to fight off potential infections. Pain pills were prescribed to compensate for the pain. I had no other choice but to suffer through it. Even though I was in recovery, it did not feel good. I had to develop a new normal. I couldn't drive. I couldn't cook for my family. I couldn't clean my house. I needed help doing everything!

> *You and your spouse have within you, everything you need to put the pieces of your marriage back together.*

What that taught me is that recovery hurts. Surviving the physical pain of adultery is one thing. But surviving the emotional pain is another. I could've avoided "the surgery" and walked away. But I chose to endure the difficult stages because I knew, one day, our marriage would walk on its own two feet again.

As JJ and I recovered, we needed rehabilitation and restoration. The same way my doctor pulled tissue from perfect ligaments to compensate for the weak areas of my foot, the Lord will bring the right reinforcements to connect you and join you the way He intended you to be. You and your spouse have within you, everything you need to put the pieces of your marriage back together. But don't allow yourself to settle in a broken place. You weren't meant to stay broken forever. You don't have to accept your painful season as your final destination. You can recover from this! Accountability, consistency and the establishment of new norms, are the antibiotics we used to prevent further infections. JJ and I went on perpetual date nights, we had frequent conversations, and we committed to making new memories until the pain converted to power.

Hurt people, Hurt people. – Most of us were taught if someone hits you, hit them back. And if someone stares at you, stare back at them. We start as early as teaching one-year old's to defend themselves by retaliating. We instill in them things like, "don't tell the teacher because the teacher does not care. Take matters into your own hands." Most of us have been preconditioned to think that we have to inflict back on others the same amount of pain they inflicted on us. Later in life, when the preacher tells us to "hold our peace and let the Lord fight our battles," or "Be still and know that God is God," we can't grasp that concept because we

have been taught that the
teacher doesn't care.

Guard your thoughts. Guard your heart. Watch your words.

Listen: I make no
excuses for people who
have done you wrong.
But this I do know; *retaliation does not work.*
Especially for husbands and wives. It will
essentially kill the marriage and the retaliation
cannot be justified. When you discovered that
your spouse had an affair, I'm sure you called
him/her names such as liar or cheater. But if
you cheat in retaliation of what they did to you,
you essentially become everything that you
once called them. This is why Proverbs ·4:23
tells us to guard ourselves and in essence, keep
ourselves from a "rebound adulterous affair."
Guard your thoughts. Guard your heart. Watch
your words. Once you start imagining yourself
with someone else for what seems like an even
"get back," your emotions will easily become
attached to a false reality. Learn to bring your
thoughts captive to the obedience of God.
If your thoughts contradict God's word and

pollute the sanctity of your marriage, Control, ALT, and Delete.

Heal together - Healing is a matter of time, but it is also a matter of opportunity. Healing should move us closer to the Healer. When you heal alone, you may achieve wholeness but your marriage will still be broken. But when you commit to healing together, you are willing to do the work as a united front. There is no microwaveable product for healing after infidelity has crept into your marriage. The un-layering of an adulterous relationship, and the trust that needs to be re-established, requires time. I remember when JJ and I were healing through our difficult season, we spent as much time together as we possibly could. Sometimes this led to having necessary conversations and other times it may have been spent building new memories with each other. Once there has been an affair, the needs and the expectations of each other will change. Once these needs are identified, be prepared to put them into action immediately. You will find a new normal. You will find that the two of you are growing closer together. Personally, I believe my husband and I act more like newlyweds now than we did in the first 5 years of our marriage. But that's only because we surrendered to the process, we were willing to do the work, and now we are reaping the benefits of marriage.

Let's pray this prayer:

Father, we invite you into our marriage today. We know that it is your will that we love one another as you love and gave up your life for us. Help us to demonstrate that same unconditional love for each other. You said that if we lack wisdom that we can ask you for it and you will give it to us generously without finding fault. So we ask for your wisdom today to give us the steps on how to put our marriage back together again. Show us how to draw in and grab hold of your word and apply your principles to our marriage. Forgive us for allowing unclean thoughts and actions to enter our minds and our hearts. We decree and declare restoration, peace of mind, and trust for our marriage. Thank you for planting sprit-filled accountability partners around us so that we can receive correction and guidance in love. We believe that you have ordained this union. We commit to loving and serving you, God, and then loving and serving each other. In Jesus' name we pray, Amen.

JJ'S JOURNEY

SURVIVING INFIDELITY

Every relationship is different. Every person reacts to pain differently. How one relationship responds to infidelity may not be the same as another. And how infidelity impacts women may be different than how infidelity impacts a man. For me, I will say this: most men can only survive infidelity once they get past the loss of their pride. As men, we take pride in what belongs to us. We take pride in the cars we drive. We take pride in the house we live in. And we take pride in the people we love. So, if my house is burglarized, or if an intruder comes in my home—and takes something valuable to me, immediately, my dignity is compromised. My self-respect is diminished—and my pride is exposed. Now I'm wondering as a man, *was*

I not enough? How did this happen on my watch?

Men internalize things. We blame ourselves. We shut down. But the truth is, a lot of what we blame ourselves for is not our fault. It's possible to protect your home, install an alarm system and still get robbed. Some things are out of your control. It's possible to do the best you can with your spouse, and still experience infidelity. The intrusion doesn't take away from you as a man. You may have done the right thing, but that doesn't mean the wrong thing can't happen.

Once you realize the truth about "how we got here", then you can do the work of rebuilding your own life as you rebuild your wife's life as well. Whether we know it or not, our wives are our home. Our relationship is our home. When infidelity happened in my marriage, I became so insecure.

I felt like I had to protect Trina against everybody. I didn't trust her interactions. I felt like everything she did with someone, was going to go somewhere else; and we were pushing each other further away from each other. What I learned during that time is one bad relationship doesn't mean every other relationship is bad. Everyone isn't trying to invade your space. And the biggest lesson I learned was: just because your spouse messes up, it doesn't mean they don't love you.

Heal Together

We are all human. We all make mistakes. This is why Hagar's situation makes sense. What Sarah and Abraham did was a mistake. They had good intentions. They just went about it the wrong way. In their mind, they were trying to see God's will done. However, they felt like they had to get involved. How many of us do the same thing? How many of us think we are doing the right thing and end up doing the wrong thing? From inception, our intentions may be pure and innocent, but at times, things will go left and end up getting out of control.

The key to bouncing back is healing together. Trina and I had to make that decision. We had to remove the scabs and allow each other to feel the pain in order to go through the healing. Many times, we expect the person to be able to make up for what has happened. But the person who hurt you can't fix you. Only God can fix you. The best thing the person can do is BE THERE while you work through it. The best thing you can do is be there as she works through it. Many times, we try to dig through the details in order to know what happened, when did it happen, and why. But the more you hear, the more you'll hurt. So make a decision to heal from where you are, not from the past that you no longer want to relive.

Trina has spoken to a lot of women who were in our shoes. As for me, I have spoken to a few men and what I've discovered is that wives need reassurance. As husbands, we have to help them with their healing. Before infidelity happened in our marriage, I used to go to certain places that I no longer go to. Why? Because I know that place represents the "reminder" of infidelity to Trina. Obviously, some places you can't avoid but I think you get the point. If a certain place or environment represents a time, place or opportunity for the same situation to happen again, give your spouse some reassurance. Make a decision that you will not allow it to happen again, and then, keep your word.

All the passcodes, phone information, everything—Trina has it. If you want to survive infidelity, you have to be transparent. Why? So, your wife or spouse can access everything. Just that level of transparency alone, will help to reassure your spouse.

When we first started to rebuild our marriage, I decided to talk to Trina all the way home when we were apart just so she knew that I wasn't rushing her off the phone to talk to anyone else. Now, I talk to her all the way home because I enjoy our conversation. Over time, my actions turned into a habit. My decision to reassure her became a place where we now bond and grow closer. Currently, Trina and I are so used to talking to each other, that it's weird when it doesn't happen. This is what I hope will happen for you. Think of ways to strengthen your marriage. Don't repeat the story. Give each other permission to heal, and no matter what, fight for your marriage. It's worth the fight.

Pardon Me

I've been on both sides of forgiveness. I have had to extend it and then there was a time when I needed it. This is why it is so important to have grace and extend forgiveness to others because you never know when you will need that same grace and forgiveness extended to you.

Having gone through our first few major hurdles in the beginning of our marriage, JJ and I thought we had climbed completely out of that era of our lives. I never could have imagined that a similar grievance would emerge from me allowing my mind to drift emotionally. It came out of nowhere (or seemingly), but I, Trina Hairston, had an emotional affair. I want to be honest with you about this because many times, people only talk about what one person in the marriage does. But the key to growth and healing is to be honest about what both parties may or may not have done.

What made this emotional affair extremely difficult to overcome is that I knew JJ struggled with forgiveness in the past. His challenges with forgiveness began when JJ was a child. So, to put him in the position to have to extend forgiveness to the one person with whom he was the most vulnerable, was a terrible decision on my part. Consequently, I needed something from him that he did not know how to give. Over time, this became a handicap in our relationship. In order to get through it, we had to rely heavily on God to help us.

> *The key to growth and healing is to be honest about what both parties may or may not have done.*

FOR-GIVE-NESS

When God thought about us and how we would need forgiveness He sent His son (Jesus) to sacrifice His life, so that when we say the words

"Father forgive me," he can, and he will. We can take a note from God's book about this. When you hear the words *"Honey, forgive me,"* realize firstly that a sacrifice has to be made. Not only on the part of the person asking for forgiveness, but also on the part of the person needing to forgive.

To some, this is a challenge, right? *I mean, let's be honest.* Why would the person (who is essentially the victim of the affair) need to sacrifice anything? Technically, they are innocent. Technically, they were done wrong. But at the same time, the word FOR-GIVE-NESS gives us a clue into why sacrifice is necessary on both sides. When you break up the word in small particles, you get FOR – GIVE – NESS.

FOR- *the sake of wholeness in my marriage,*
I am willing to ***GIVE*** *up my right to be angry and bruised by what has happened*
*so that we can become the full (**NESS**) of what marriage is supposed to exemplify.*

> *The longer you stay in the mirage of negative feelings, the harder it will be to climb out and make the decision to forgive.*

JJ had a right to be angry, upset, hurt and bruised. It was even healthy to allow him to feel those emotions. It was not healthy, however, for him stay hidden in those emotions. Why? Because the longer you stay in the mirage of negative feelings, the harder it will be to climb out and make the decision to forgive. Moreover, for believers, it is necessary to forgive.

Matthew 6:15 tells us that if we do not forgive others then our heavenly Father will not forgive us. In other words, to the degree that we *need* forgiveness, we must be willing to *extend* forgiveness. Forgiveness is mentioned over 100 times in the Bible. Do you see how much emphasis God puts on the act of forgiveness? If forgiving someone can allow you access to the kind of mercy

> *Forgiveness is not just about freeing others; it's also about freeing yourself.*

and freedom that you will inevitably need, then unforgiveness is the umbilical cord that will keep you bound to your sinful nature. Forgiveness is not just about freeing others; it's also about freeing yourself.

I had to accept a hard truth in order to receive forgiveness. First, I had to accept that I was the one who had done something wrong, and this was extremely difficult for me. The realization of my culpability brought me to such a low place. I had learned how to repent to God, but now I had to repent to my husband. I had to admit that I did wrong, and make an active decision to turn away from my wrong actions. To ensure that I did not dig myself in an unending hole of guilt, I needed to find a way to lift myself up. I almost fell into depression because the guilt was that strong, but I am determined not to be that person. Immediately, I went into recovery mode in order to restore myself. I found songs to sing and prayers to pray to keep me lifted. For a few weeks, I walked around our home singing,

"I'm not going back, I'm moving ahead, I'm here to declare to you my past is over in you, all things are made new, surrender my life to Christ, I'm moving forward...

After repeating scriptures to lift myself up (over and over again) and after singing motivational songs, and encouraging myself, I was ready to move on quickly. Isn't it interesting how we tend to want life to speed up when we are feeling guilty and judged? Without saying the words to our spouses, our attitudes can unknowingly and unintentionally reflect, "Get Over It"! Now, don't get me wrong. I am all for self-empowerment and lifting yourself up. It is certainly necessary. However, when you are guilty of a wrongdoing, you need to spend just as much time repairing the other person, too. Here I was, lifting up Trina, but what about my husband? What about the man that I hurt? JJ was broken. While I was singing, "I'm moving forward," and while I was busy worshipping my way out of this guilt, JJ was still wounded.

When I saw him doing his daily routine, I could tell that he was somewhat in a debilitated state. I couldn't leave him where he was. In order for our marriage to heal, it was time for me to leave my gift at the altar and be reconciled.

> *The Holy Spirit doesn't just give you the power to shout; He also gives you the conviction to stop.*

Many of us need disciplinary action or exposure to get us together. But I long for the day when we don't have to be "sat down by the church" because of our sin, but instead, we will sit ourselves down. I long for the day when we decide not to go to rehearsal, not to go out with our friends, and not to give our time to social media, and instead, use that time to restore and rebuild our spouses so that we can work toward reconciliation. The Holy Spirit doesn't just give you the power to shout; He also gives you the conviction to stop. I had to stop all extra-curricular activities and focus on my marriage. I didn't just want to worship at the altar by myself. I wanted my husband at the altar singing "Moving forward" with me.

Humble. Pray. Turn. Seek. Heal.

If my people, which are called by my name, shall humble themselves, and pray, and seek my face, and turn from their wicked ways; then will I hear from heaven, and will forgive their sin, and will heal their land. – 2 Chronicles 7:14

Here is the pattern to follow for those who need forgiveness. Notice all of these words represent an action that needs to take place. 2 Chronicles 7:14 says this: If my people who are called by my name would **Humble** themselves.

It is amazing to me that God would start by mentioning the need for us to humble ourselves. Although the Bible does not indicate that there is significance to the sequential order in which these words are listed, I believe there is meaning to everything in the Bible. *Really*

God? You would want us to humble ourselves before we pray, before we turn, and before we seek? Yes. God cares about our posture, not just our prayers. Humility takes away the idea that you can handle it on your own. Humility gives God full access to help you to clean up the mess you have created. The unspoken rule says "If you broke it, you fix it" but that is not the umbrella God places us under. God is so gracious that if we break it, he will also help us to fix it!

I love that so much about God! I love that when we have been called to the carpet on something, we may jump to defense, offense, excuses or finger-pointing. But God jumps to love, forgiveness, reconciliation and patience. Our reactions are rooted in pride. But God's compassion is clothed in humility. Literally and intentionally, God wants us to put on humility like a piece of clothing so that our pride will not be indecently exposed. Every day, particularly when we have done wrong, we should die to whatever our flesh is instructing us to do and submit with humility to God and to our spouse.

Humility says I can't handle it on my own:

I am guilty of trying to handle everything on my own. I am the type of person who will drive home after grocery shopping with 10 bags, most of them being heavy; and instead of calling for help from my husband or children, I will burden myself by putting 4 bags on one arm, 4 bags on the other arm and one in each hand. I will struggle to close and open doors, and I will limp my way to the counter if I have to—but no matter what, I determine to get all of this done in one trip.

But there is another option. Humility instead of Pride. What if I utilized the help I had in the house, to free me of the heavy load? It's funny how we say "God won't put more on us than we can handle," but there are something's that we have willingly taken on. Yet, He still does not expect us to handle it without his help.

Now that your relationship is in this state, it would be extremely difficult for you to fix your personal brokenness (your inner self), clean up the mistakes you have made, and repair the fragmented pieces of your spouse's heart—all by yourself. You would look like me, with 10 bags in your hand, struggling to get in the door. This is why God says for us to humble ourselves. Humility gives God permission to grab the door and help you out because you accept "I can't do this without Him." Not only will this lighten your load, but God will also give you the grace to carry what you are capable of holding.

Consider Others

The greatest attribute about someone who is humble is that they seek to make sure the other person is taken care of more than themselves. Philippians 2:3 says in humility we should consider others more important than ourselves. This does not leave you out or make you less of a person. It just means you should make it a priority to see to it that your spouse is in a

> *Every day and throughout the day, your goal should be to feed your marriage.*

healthy place. You should make sure your spouse is good, and trust that they will make sure you are good. If your spouse is in touch or not, know that God will take care of you because He shows favor to the humble. It is totally in line with God's word to become so humble that your actions reflect the desire to restore your spouse and to repair the damage you have caused. Every day and throughout the day, your goal should be to feed your marriage. Do whatever it takes in that moment to pour life back into your spouse. Questions like *what can I do for you today to lighten your load?* Or, *what can I do to assure you that I am re-committed to this marriage?* Although your spouse may not have an immediate answer, it is the act of humility that will live long in their hearts.

If my people who are called by my name would humble themselves and pray..

I wish I could have suited up like a medical doctor, opened up JJ's heart and performed surgery. I would've removed all the hurt and pain that I had caused (and any other hurt that had been there from his own life experiences). I honestly wish it was that easy. But the truth is, forgiveness isn't a microwaveable fix. A lot of the work that needed to be done was going to require my efforts, and the majority of it had to be done through prayer.

One of the greatest things about marriage is that no one can pray for your spouse the way you can. Yes, even though your actions caused the pain, God still sees the two of you as one. Although there may be a strain in your natural relationship, there is a spiritual connection that can reach the heart of your spouse with God being your mediator. This example can be seen in the way God loves us. When we turn from him, he still gives us the ministry of reconciliation. Which means, your prayers of restoration, reconciliation and healing for your spouse all line up with God's word. And whatever we ask

---

Praying in the spirit is one of the most powerful weapons you can use.

according to his will He hears us.

We should also pray in the spirit. We make light of speaking in tongues as if it is a punchline to a joke, but on the contrary. Praying in the spirit is one of the most powerful weapons you can use. Especially in the circumstances where you are not in the controlling seat as it pertains to the life or death of your marriage. When we pray naturally, we can become lost for words, or we may not be saying in human language the words that God wants us to say. But when we pray in the spirit, he intercedes for us and he pleads (to the Father) for us (Romans 8:26). And since we know that it is God's will for us to be reconciled to each other, by praying in the spirit, you can intercede for your spouse according to the will of God. Who is more qualified or more connected to your spouse than you? Praying is the best tool you can use for what seems to be an uphill battle of forgiveness and reconciliation. Not only that, but prayer is vital to your own sanity. As I explained previously, coming to the realization of what you have done can be painstaking for you to handle on your own. But pray. Pray in English and pray in the Spirit. Keep yourself encouraged through prayer.

> ***If my people who are called by name would humble themselves, pray, and seek my face.***

So here is some full disclosure for you. Since JJ and I moved into our current home (about 3 years ago at the time of this writing), I had not cleaned out my closet. There were items that I felt like were lost amongst the mountains of clothes that I had acquired. So recently it dawned on me that there was a specific item that I needed. I decided to clean out my entire closet in search of one specific item. And what I discovered was revelatory! The item *itself* was not lost. It was where I had originally laid it—still folded up the way I had folded it. The problem was, I had placed so many things in front of it and on top of it, I couldn't see it any longer.

> *Clean up the closet of your heart and mind. Make seeking the face of God your priority.*

This example is exactly what we do to God. We place ideas, desires, social media, schedules and even people before Him. And when we find ourselves in a sunken position, we realize that there is a deficit deep in our souls. It almost feels like we have wandered off so far that we can't see God anymore. But if we were to clear our mind and seek his face, and seek his desire for our lives, we will find that he is right where he always was. He is waiting for us.

Seeking the face of God requires an effort on our part. It is easier to look to trusted friends and family members when you are facing hard times. But, if we would make a conscious effort to humble ourselves, pray, and seek His face, we will find that God is there. Truthfully, if we had been seeking his face, we would not have had time to entertain the desires that caused us to be in that state in the first place!

When we seek his face, we yield and say, "Lord, not my will but your will be done in my life." My recommendation to you would be to clean up the closet of your heart and mind. Make seeking the face of God your priority. Even before you take action to repair your marriage, Seek God's face. Remember: *if we draw nigh unto him he will draw nigh to us.*

Turn from your wicked ways

Here is where spirituality meets practicality. To think that you can still keep company with the things and the people that played a hand in your downfall, is ludicrous. Someone once said that the definition of insanity is doing the same thing and expecting different results. We all know that this is not the literal meaning of insanity, but it would be insane to think that the enemy won't play on your weaknesses. Nothing about your life can resemble the things that you participated in, which caused you to fall. Part of taking responsibility for your actions is realizing that being a changed person will be vital to the survival of your marriage. I can say with certainty, your spouse needs to see

> *Most of the actions that become destructive to our marriage start with a thought.*

change more than hear about how you are going to change. To make these changes, you are going to have to set up measures to guard yourself. Become less reactive and more proactive in guarding your environment. My husband and I have become increasingly aware of our surroundings. Out of respect for ourselves and the marriage, there are places we won't go, and people we will not interact with, deliberately. Behavior that leads to the destruction of our marriage is unacceptable.

Moreover, we should guard our minds. Most of the actions that become destructive to our marriage start with a thought. Un-tamed thoughts become fantasies. Eventually, you will begin to create these scenarios in your mind. And given the opportunity, your actions will follow what you have fanaticized about. So turn from your wicked ways, fill your heart and your mind with things that are pleasing to both God and your spouse.

If my people who are called by my name would humble themselves and pray, seek my face, and turn from their wicked ways then I will hear from heaven, forgive their sins and heal.

If you hear a fire alarm, what do you do? If you hear a baby cry what is your response? When someone can hear, they can make a decision and respond accordingly. Let's just face it, when someone is angry, you can do a lot of talking, but unless they can see that change has taken place in your life, they probably won't be able to hear and respond with forgiveness. Ultimately, forgiveness speaks in a language that can only be heard when there is action associated with it. The action in this scripture is to pray, seek, and turn. The action needed for forgiveness in your marriage, won't be much different. It will take humility. It will also take prayer to our Father and communication (including some tough conversations) with your spouse. It will take seeking God's face, but also, you will need to put your spouse first and find out what *their* needs are. It will take turning away from your wicked ways, but it is also going to take establishing some healthy routines and practices. All of these (and more) need to be in place so that your spouse can hear and respond with forgiveness, reconciliation and healing

Your spouse will be able to forgive you when he or she feels safe with you. When they can see that your relationship with Christ is what has humbled you and caused you to be in right standing, they will let that wall down.

Perhaps your particular circumstance was not an affair (emotional or physical). But even still, this scripture still applies. *Pray, Seek, Turn, for the sake of Hearing, Forgiveness and Healing in your life and in your marriage.*

Here are a list of practical things that can be done in addition:

- Be willing to have touch conversations-
  - ○ It would not be fair to shut down or give limited answers. Be willing to communicate your feelings.
- Be accountable-
  - ○ Commit to being where you say you are going to be, when you say you are

going to be there. The only spontaneous occurrences should be ones that promote the togetherness of you and your spouse.

- Check in-
  - ○ Don't assume your spouse knows where you are. When you are apart from each other, Facetime him/her.
- Include and give access-
  - ○ Your spouse should not only have an open invitation to wherever you may be, but you should bring them with you whenever possible.
  - ○ There should not be any hidden areas of your life. Including cell phone, passwords, and/or hangouts.
- Build new memories together-
  - ○ For every bad thought your spouse may have, seize that moment to create a new memory. This could be as simple as a kiss, hug, alone time, date. You should help contribute whatever is necessary to combat any bad thoughts they may have.

- Be Patient-
  - You cannot place a time limit on someone's healing. You can only promise to hold their hand and walk them through to complete healing.
- Seek Counsel-
  - You need to have a trusted un-biased person that both of you agree to help you walk through this process.
- Touch often-
  - You would be surprised how much physical contact builds a relationship. Hold hands, a gentle hug, a nice back massage; all of these things lead to bonding and tearing down walls of separation.
- Close all doors-
  - Whoever has access to you that is not in agreement and full support of your marriage, can no longer be a part of your life. Close all doors that will lead to any negative talk of the two of you coming back together.

PARDON ME

I grew up in a family who held grudges. We literally would take pride in it. We were known for our walk with God, and we were known for other things as well, but one of the major things they said about the Hairston's was, don't cross them. Forgiveness has always been a challenge for me, and a lot of it stems from my childhood. My father and I had an estranged relationship. He never forgave my mother for divorcing him. My parents divorced when I was 3 years old and I didn't see my father again until I was 10. My father distanced himself from the entire family. And my grandfather divorced his wife as well. So, I learned, through my family members, how to respond to people who do you wrong: *cut them off.* Don't speak to them. Keep on moving as if nothing happened. *They'll be OK.* This was my training pre-marriage. So, when Trina and I found ourselves on a rocky road, I figured we would do what my father and grandfather did. I cut her off. I backed away. I shut down.

Even though I had done wrong in our marriage, I worked to fix it. But when I was done wrong, my first response was to walk away because that's what I saw. Many people are products of their environment. Some people act out of character because they don't know any better. But the turning point for me was when I realized who Trina truly was. Trina meant too much for me to walk away. Trina wasn't just any woman—and several people told me how easy it would be to find someone else. The reality is, I'd never find another Trina. I'd never find another woman who would pray for me when I was going through, who would build me up when I failed, who would care for my heart and our children. No one came close to Trina. So I had to deal with it. I had to deal with the hurt and anger. I had to deal with the pain of it all.

I decided to not give up on her and not give up on us.

I could've stayed and tormented her, but I realized that the more I talked about it and the more we brought it up, it would hurt us both. I wanted to linger in that negative space for a while, because of how I grew up, but one day, I decided to let it go. At our worst, we were living in separate houses. Even when we lived in the same house, we had become so separated, it felt like I was living alone. Don't let that happen to your marriage. It's a terrible way to live. Some days, you're going to have to do the hard thing: forgive her. If you don't, you will hurt yourself. You see, most people see forgiveness as "a get out of jail free card." So, if we forgive them, we are letting them get away with murder. But forgiveness works the opposite way. True forgiveness allows you to become vulnerable enough to admit you are hurt and at the same time free yourself. Once you release yourself you can begin to heal. Unforgiveness keeps you trapped in a wall of hurt. It traps you in the same space as your hurt. Once I was able to forgive

Trina, then she was able to be there for me. Until that moment happened, unforgiveness separated us. What is separating you from being close to your spouse? Is it a grudge? Disappointment? A secret? Whatever it is, let it go—and let it go quickly.

My 3 steps to forgiveness are simple:

1. Decide to NOT bring up what happened.
   - This may be hard to do at first, but every time you bring it up, you open the wound again. Every time you discuss it (after you've already faced it), you add more visual details to your mind; and men never forget that. Don't allow yourself to slip into that place. It isn't healthy and it isn't helpful.
2. Decide NOT to rehearse what happened in your head.
   - Our brain has the ability to store a lot of memory. The most painful thoughts are on constant replay. Do not rehearse the scene in your head. Do not replay or re-read the messages. If you do, you will get more

upset with the person and forget that this is bigger than you. The enemy doesn't want your marriage to work. The person was used by the enemy, but the person isn't the enemy. Guard your heart and your mind, and delete anything that would cause you to slip back.

3. Decide to LOVE in spite of the hurt.
    - I know this sounds like a tall order, but one day you will need forgiveness too. One day, I needed Trina to look past my faults, and love me despite my mistakes. We reap what we sow. Don't pretend to be somewhere you are not. Be honest with your spouse about what you need. But don't put up a wall because that will make it impossible for her to come close.

Once I was able to forgive Trina, it released her to love me and help me through the process. Your spouse needs your help to forgive. Help her. Help him. And win together.

RESTORING TRUST

In 2004, Universal Pictures released a widely popular movie titled *Ray,* which details the life and career of the legendary rhythm and blues musician, Ray Charles. The movie starred Jamie Foxx, Regina King, and Kerry Washington; earned $75 million in the USA, and 124 million worldwide. It also claimed 2 Oscars and 52 additional awards. Admittedly, I have watched *Ray* several times. I am fascinated by the acting, the storytelling and well, Ray's blindness. One of the most fascinating details about Ray Charles was that, even though he could not see, he learned how to rely on other senses in order to help him get through life. No doubt, Ray Charles was blind, but he also had a keen sense of hearing. He even used his sense of touch to make necessary observations and this allowed him to paint a vivid picture in his mind's eye. I imagine that Ray even used his sense of smell to determine how to move from place to place, in order to keep himself out harm's way.

It is common knowledge that when someone loses a sensory function, like eyesight, the areas of the brain devoted to that nonfunctioning sensory are rewired to empower another part of the body. The more I think about that truth, in comparison to the movie *Ray,* the more I see a connection to marriage and trust. When trust is broken in one's marriage, this causes an impairment of some sort. Mistrust then reinforces a kind of blindness, and all of a sudden, things you used to see, feel and understand about your spouse have now become a gray area of distrust. So how do you function?

How do you remain in the marriage without having to be glued to each other 24/7 just to make sure it doesn't happen again? How do you hear the alerts from

Which senses do you lean on now that your sense of trust is broken?

a cell phone and not be tempted to look at his phone to see who is texting him? How do you know that when she says she's going out with her girlfriends that she is actually telling the truth? Which senses do you lean on now that your sense of trust is broken?

Rewiring is Necessary

Just like Ray Charles had to adapt his life to compensate for his loss of sight, you will have to learn to rewire all of your broken sensors and simply trust God. That's first. Trust was broken by your spouse, but trust was not broken in God. At the end of the day, God must remain your "go-to" sensory option, when all else fails. God must be the place where you turn when you are overwhelmed, nervous, anxious or paranoid. In addition, you and your spouse will have to safeguard the relationship. Install an alarm system in your marital house (metaphorically speaking) and don't give the code to anyone else but your spouse. Imagine that your marriage is a home, and someone who is handicapped now lives there. In order to accommodate the disabled person, you will need to build a walkway, perhaps install an elevator, or shift the sink and tub to make sure the handicap person can reach the essentials in your home. In the same way, your marriage needs to think about the new accommodations you will need to install, and the cost associated with it. This is the only way to repair a broken marriage and rebuild security back in your relationship.

Typically, when you do not trust someone, everything they tell you will seem sketchy. And you will become extremely skeptical. It is human nature to mentally weigh what the person is saying based on what we think the outcome of the situation will be. We have been programed to follow our gut instincts. When trust has been broken your gut feelings will rationalize and make decisions purely based on past experiences and fear (fear of the unknown and known). When trust has been broken, your brain will rationalize and make decisions purely based on past experiences and fear (fear of the unknown or known). However, the blueprint to learning to trust again is not found in your gut but it is found in Proverbs 3:5-6. Trust in the Lord with all of your heart. Lean not to your own understanding. In all your ways acknowledge him and he will direct your path. This scripture

> *Your marriage will be restored, once you place your trust in the one who brought you together in the first place.*

answers the question on how to rest in trusting God when you don't know how to trust your spouse. Your marriage will be restored, once you place your trust in the one who brought you together in the first place. And over time, as you recover and rebuild, trust will be restored.

Navigating the Unknown

Let's go back to the beginning once more. In Genesis, God told Adam not to eat from a particular tree: the tree of the knowledge of good and evil. The enemy came in, however, and deceived Eve. He coerced her to eat of that tree, and she did it—not because she was hungry. Not because she needed something to eat. But because she was

> *When we ignore God's instructions to feed our needs, we will always go blind.*

deceived into thinking that the tree would give her access to something she needed to know. As if God would hide something from us that he knew was important, the enemy always introduces deception with a lie. Eve became curious and took the bait. Even though God gave specific instructions, Eve did it anyway. When we ignore God's instructions to feed our needs, we will always go blind. Eve went blind in the area of trust. Eve also lost touch with God and her closeness to Adam. The moment they sinned, they knew they were naked and became ashamed. Sin always brings shame, and shame always brings blame. Adam blamed Eve. Eve blamed the serpent, and the story continued until God had to step in.

When I think about that story in relationship to marriage, I believe that God designed an area, in our human existence, where we do not have all the answers. That space of the unknown is exactly the place where God wanted us to depend on him. And in all of our uncertainties, God created us to long for him and develop a hunger after him so that he could

> *Because I am led by the Holy Spirit, I can rest in knowing that God has me.*

direct us and instruct us. The benefit of this would be that we would learn to lean on him for direction, and not our own understanding. My advice would be to stop trying to figure it out and trust God.

Finding the Truth

One thing I know for sure is this: following the path of God will lead you into all truth. So, if there is a truth (not a guess, not a gut instinct) but a truth to be found, the Holy Spirit will lead and guide you. In my season of distrust, my mother would always instruct me to trust God. She would say, "If there is something you need to know, He will reveal it to you. If it has not been revealed yet, it is simply not my season to know." Because of these wise words I decided that there was no need for me to plan stake-outs. I decided not to look at my husband's phone every time it rang or obsess over being next to him for reasons of distrust. *Because I am led by the Holy Spirit, I can rest in knowing that God has me.* The same is true for you. God has you. God knows you. And when the time comes for you to know, He will reveal it and give you the power to endure it.

Let me end this chapter with a personal story. I really want you to understand how trusting God works. When JJ and I were going through our "season of uncertainty", he told me that he was done with living a separate life, and he had asked God to forgive him. He asked for my forgiveness as well. Then he talked to my son (who was about 8 years old at the time) and told him that life was going to get better for us as a family. He started to repair all of the broken relationships with friends and family that had been compromised due to the contention in our marriage. His actions told me that he was serious. There was a different aura about him. His focus was on one thing: getting his life and his family back together. However, this did not happen overnight. There was still a period of time where we lived in two separate homes. We were healing and repairing, but all the while, I was determined to trust God. The Holy Spirit had given me the peace I needed. In addition, JJ was accountable to us. JJ gave me a timeline. Everything that he said he was going to do, he did it when he said he would. I didn't have to ask any questions, he offered the information. He began to invite me into his space, his heart, and his thoughts. These things were happening prior to us physically living in the same home again.

So, I say that to say this: you will know when the time is right to trust your spouse. Not only will God give you that peace, but you will see all of the signs that confirm what is being said. My advice is to be patient, trust God, and He will ultimately lead you into trusting your spouse again.

RESTORING TRUST

Now that I'm older, I know a little more than I did when I was a kid. All of us do. So if someone were to ask me what I would've done differently, I would begin by saying: very few people make an intentional decision to cheat. Usually, we end up in a situation that moved "left" very quickly. And most of us don't cheat with people we've never met. Usually, we cheat with people we have been around and found comfort in.

As trust is rebuilt in a marriage, both parties must become more conscious of the people they are around. I had to make better decisions about who I let into my personal space, and I had to be OK if Trina asked why they were there.

Here is another hard lesson that took me a while to accept. If you have people in your space

who are not satisfied with themselves, 9 times
out of 10, they will try to sabotage your life too.
Hurt people hurt people, and everyone doesn't
want to see you win. Some people look for your
misery to give them company. But trust is a non-
negotiable and anyone who compromises your
covenant, doesn't deserve your company.

Trina and I have made a conscious decision
to restore our marriage. Now that we are better,
I make sure that Trina approves anyone who is
coming in my space. And she allows me to do
the same. Above all, trust is crucial. Sometimes,
our spouse is trust-worthy but the person (she
is hanging around), isn't safe. The person doesn't
edify marriage. The person is reckless. These
individuals need to be removed from your circle.
It doesn't mean you can't do life with them, but
for some, you must learn to love them from a
distance.

Anytime, Trina and I had an issue happen
in our marriage with other people, it always
began from a pure place. They were cool. They
were polite. They were helpful. Then, a good

thing turned into a bad thing. So, now that I'm older, I would tell my younger self: don't overestimate your strengths and under-estimate your weaknesses. All of us can become distracted if we are not paying attention.

If I could do it all over again, I would make sure that Trina trusted everyone who was around me. I would've paid attention to those who celebrated my marriage, and those who didn't. Admittedly, I ignored a lot of red flags because I figured Trina was just being insecure. But she was connected. She could see what I couldn't see. And the worst thing a man has to face is when his wife says something is going to happen, and it happens just like she said it would!

Finally, if I could do it all over again, I would've been more transparent with Trina about what I felt and what I wanted (as a husband). Trina and I grew up together. We were kids when we started "dating." I was 14 going on 15. Trina was 13 going on 14. I was too young to be honest with her. I wasn't even honest with myself. But that trickled down into our marriage. I withheld from her, in the beginning because I felt like she would judge me. Now, I know that she and I had some of the same desires, and we just didn't know it. I wish I would have trusted her (sooner) with what I wanted and not assume she would leave me or become turned off by the real me.

All was not lost. Trina and I grew together. In every area of our marriage—physically, emotionally, spiritually, sexually—we made a decision to grow together. I stopped fearing if Trina would shoot down a "crazy idea," and started trusting that she could handle anything I said to her.

As I end this chapter, I want you to know that restoration is possible. Most people see Trina and I now, but they don't see the days when I told her to delete her Facebook app from her phone. They don't see the days when I was afraid that if someone contacted her, it would lead to something else. Fear never fixes a problem— if anything, it makes things worse. What fixes the problem is trust. And trust is believing in something you cannot control. You can't control your wife. You have to *choose* to trust her. Your wife can't control you. She has to choose to trust you. If you give yourself some time to get through this rough patch, you will experience joy in a marriage that you didn't think possible. Trust me. Your best days are ahead of you, because God is a miracle-worker!

ABOUT TRINA HAIRSTON

Trina's life began with church and music. Her father, Bishop JC White, was the director and songwriter for the renowned Institutional Radio Choir in Brooklyn NY. Bishop White moved to Connecticut to Pastor a church. It was at that church that Trina would meet JJ Hairston and they began dating at the age of 14 and 15 years old. Without any counseling, JJ and Trina eloped to the City Town Hall and got married at the age of 18 and 19. The secrecy of their then tumultuous marriage began to show signs of quick deterioration. Trina began to rely on the faith that had been instilled in her since birth to help repair this broken relationship. "I heard countless testimonies and sermons of God's healing power from the ugliest of diseases, however when it came to my marriage, I was advised from the church to divorce and I refused. Healing was for my marital issues, too," says Trina. By the grace of God, Trina and JJ have been married for 25+ years and have now started the ministry, Amazing Love, which teaches the God designed road map to a successful and happy marriage. Together they are raising 3 children and recently relocated to the Maryland area where they both serve on the leadership staff at City of Praise Family Ministries under the great leadership of Bishop Joel and Co-Pastor YLawnda Peebles.

In addition to singing with and Co-Leading the ministry of JJ Hairston and Youthful Praise, the couple recently started an independent record label, JamesTown Music, where Trina serves as VP of Radio and Media. In addition, Trina has obtained her certifications to teach the good news of Marriage and Reconciliation through the American Association of Christian Counselors, Light University, Dr.'s Les and Leslie Parrot's SYMBIS program, and she is certified by Jimmy and Karen Evans to teach Marriage Today and Marriage on the Rock material. Trina is currently enrolled at University of Maryland University college where she is pursuing her degree in Psychology.

About J.J. Hairston

J.J. Hairston and Youthful Praise (affectionately known as YP) continue to make waves in the Gospel Music Industry while garnering national and international recognition. Founded in 1991, the once 35-member church choir from Bridgeport, CT has transformed into a Billboard chart topping national gospel artist.

Recently, J.J. Hairston & YP have garnered much success with the release of "You Deserve It," an infectious worship song that has taken the nation by storm.

The single was named #1 in 2017 by Billboard Magazine on four charts: The Hot Gospel Songs Chart, Hot Gospel Song Artists Chart, the Gospel Air Play Chart, and the Gospel Digital Songs Chart.

This year Hairston and the group have won 6 Stellar Gospel Music Awards, a Billboard Music Award, and an ASCAP Rhythm & Soul Award. JJ Hairston and Youthful Praise were also nominated for a 2018 GRAMMY for Best Gospel Performance/Song.

JJ Hairston is the new CEO and founder of Jamestown Music. This new label is exclusively distributed by Nashville-based Entertainment One. Hairston's goal is to continue to develop music through this new venture that can be used as a tool for audiences everywhere to develop their personal relationship with God.

About Amazing Love

JJ and Trina Hairston, founders of Amazing Love, have been married for 24 years. Their love story began in 1989. Just into their teenage years they already knew that they would be together forever. In July of 1994 they secretly eloped to the town clerk's office in Bridgeport CT. and said their nuptials. They remained secretly married for about 6 months before the relationship began to suffer, as they did not have any pre-marital counseling. As word began to spread about their marriage, the advice given to them was that they should divorce. God's Amazing Love manifested in their relationship and they decided to put the pieces of the marriage back together again.

Amazing Love was founded in 2013. This mentorship program identifies the areas in where marital relationships will essentially grow. Whether you are engaged, newlyweds, or seasoned in marriage, Amazing Love has a program for you. We are building lasting marriages and teaching the principles of the type of Love that endures.

Amazing Love offers:
Pre-Marital Mentorship
Mentorship in maintaining a healthy Marriage
Marriage Intensive Care (MICU) for the broken marriages

One-on-One Marriage education
Seminars
Conferences
Retreats

Acknowledgements

God, THANK YOU! *For we know that all things work together for the good of those who love God and are called according to his purpose.*

Father, out of all of the countless minutes, hours, days, months and years that I doubted myself, you would not let me give up. You always sent an encouraging reminder of the assignment you have given me. I believe you strategically placed the right situations, (some good and some evil) and the right people, (some moral and some corrupt) in my life to push me to this moment. You are certainly omnipresent.

You knew in 1994 that I was pregnant with a story. A story that would teach me who you are and a story that I could be used as a witnessing tool to help someone else in 2019 and beyond.

I pray that the same anointing that was on my life when you cradled me in your arms would permeate through the pages of this book and encourage, stabilize and build up every husband and wife who is in need of your MIRACLE WORKING POWER.

He/She that hath a listening ear, let that person hear this book. Let them be planted in you, and KNOW that you are a marriage miracle worker!

To my husband and best friend, James (JJ), Look what the Lord has done for us and through us. We had no idea that our story would become a book. We were just trying to survive. Thank you for being obedient to God. I am so IN LOVE with you. If we had to do it all over again, I'd still choose you. Thank you for having patience with me and thank you for calming my franticness! God knew I needed you. Thank you for believing in me and for your willingness to always share your platform with me. As long as you keep following Christ, I will always follow you!

To my children, James IV, Janay, and Jayelle: I am so IN LOVE with each of you. Thank you for your patience with me. Thank you for your encouraging words and for pushing me to do all the things that I should have done before you were born. God knew that I needed you in my life and I thank him for trusting me to guide you in this world. I want you to do even greater than I have done. Start now!

To my Dad and Mom, I don't know if I will ever be able to adequately express how much your presence on earth as my parents, has meant to me. You both are the epitome of greatness, and the personification of Godly examples. You embody integrity, grace, and everything that I desire to be. I'll spend the rest of my life letting you know how much I love you.

Shaun! When we started 4 (plus) years ago, I had no idea that I was speaking to someone who would ultimately become a best friend. You know all of my secrets, yet you never judged me or looked at me any differently. In fact, you did just the opposite. You pushed me to greatness and to the finish line. I am in awe of your wisdom and your ability to translate my heart's thoughts. God knew both of our stories and planted something in us that would eventually bring us to the moment we met. Instantly, we became graphed into each other's lives. I'm so grateful. Thank You!

To our Pastor's, Bishop Joel and Ylawnda Peebles. Where do we start? Thank you for all of your wisdom and guidance. Your example has caused us to be better people. We are so grateful that God allowed us to be a part of your lives, and then a part of the City of Praise Family (emphasis on Family) Ministries. Our lives will never ever, never ever ever be the same again!

Youthful Praise, some of you have had a front row seat to the good and the not so good times, but look what the Lord has done. We pray that the same favor that has been graced upon our lives be given to you in multiplicity.

To all of our family and friends—Thank You for your support and prayers.

Contact information for booking:
Halo Management
Melanie Pratt
melanie@halomanagementgroup.com
704-965-5440

Certified Marriage Coach
Amazing Love
amazinglove.love

Made in the USA
Middletown, DE
28 April 2023